SHORT WAL
MADE EASY

LOCH LOMOND
AND
THE TROSSACHS

Ordnance
Survey

Contents

Walk 1

BALLOCH

Distance
2.7 miles / 4.3km

Time
1½ hours

GO BY TRAIN
CATCH A BUS

Start/Finish
Balloch

Parking G83 8LQ
Moss o' Balloch
car park

Cafés/pubs
Balloch

Beautiful parkland
and stunning
gardens; birds
of prey and
aquarium

Moss o' Balloch
Plantations

Page 14

  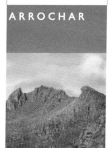

Walk 5	Walk 6	Walk 7
TYNDRUM	**KILLIN**	**KINGSHOUSE TO LOCHEARNHEAD**

Distance
3.6 miles/5.7km

Time
2 hours

Start/Finish
Dalrigh

Parking FK20 8RX
Tyndrum Community
Woodland car park

Cafés/pubs
Tyndrum

Distance
3.4 miles/5.5km

Time
2 hours

Start/Finish
Killin

Parking FK21 8TE
Car park off Lyon
Road

Cafés/pubs
Killin

Distance
3.6 miles/5.7km

Time
2 hours

Start Kingshouse
Finish Lochearnhead

Parking FK19 8QG
Lochearnhead car park

Cafés/pubs
Kingshouse;
Balquhidder Station;
Lochearnhead

**Delightful wood-
land; historic
battle site;
old gold mine;
Tyndrum**

**Memorable Falls
of Dochart; Loch
Tay views; legend
of Fingal**

**Majestic mountain
scenery and
beautiful native
woodland**

Walk 8

THREE BRIDGES OF CALLANDER

Distance
4.6 miles/7.3km

Time
2½ hours   CATCH A BUS

Start/Finish
Callander

Parking FK17 8BA
Callander Meadows
car park, Leny Road

Cafés/pubs
Callander; Kilmahog

Lovely water
meadow; Iron Age
hillfort; Roman
fort; Samson's
Putting Stone

Walk 9

BRIG O' TURK

Distance
2.2 miles/3.5km

Time
1¼ hours   CATCH A BUS

Start/Finish
Glen Finglas Gateway
Centre, Brig o' Turk

Parking FK17 8HR
Lendrick Hill car park,
Brig o' Turk

Cafés/pubs
Brig o' Turk Tearoom;
Byre Inn, Brig o' Turk

Bicycle Tree; *The
39 Steps* location;
magical children's
playground

Walk 10

WATERFALLS AND OAK COPPICE TRAILS

Distance
1.9 miles/3.1km

Time
1 hour   CATCH A BUS

Start/Finish
The Lodge Forest
Visitor Centre

Parking FK8 3SX
The Lodge car park

Cafés/pubs
The Lodge Café;
Aberfoyle

Impressive
waterfalls;
Lumberjills
memorial; red
squirrels, roe deer

GETTING OUTSIDE IN LOCH LOMOND AND THE TROSSACHS

" "

revel in a
wilderness
adventure on
Inchcailloch, an
island in Loch
Lomond

OS Champion
Bee Leask

Cruising on Loch Lomond, Balloch

A very warm welcome to the new Short Walks Made Easy guide to Loch Lomond and the Trossachs – what a fantastic selection of leisurely walks we have for you!

Loch Lomond and the Trossachs National Park is one of the great outdoor treasures of Scotland. Travelling from the south, the stunning mountain scenery surrounding sparkling Loch Lomond is barely 20 miles from Glasgow. While the national park was established in 2002, as a visitor destination it has been popular since mid-Victorian times. This is partly due to its proximity to Glasgow, but also through the writing of Sir Walter Scott whose prose conjured a literary magic in his portrayal of Rob Roy country, creating an intoxicating infusion of glorious scenery, history and mythology that continues to ignite imaginations.

Centred on Loch Lomond, Britain's largest loch, and the Great Trossachs Forest – the country's biggest national nature reserve – walks in this guide follow a selection of easy-going paths throughout the national park. Relax in landscaped parkland at Balloch Castle and revel in a wilderness adventure on Inchcailloch, an island in Loch Lomond. You can witness memorable cascades at the Falls of Dochart, extensive views over Loch Long and Loch Tay, and awe-inspiring mountain vistas featuring Ben Lomond and the Arrochar Alps. Enjoy woodland wanders at Tyndrum and Aberfoyle, stroll around the delightful conservation village of Luss, and keep a lookout for red squirrels, red deer and birds of prey.

Bee Leask, OS Champion

WE SMILE MORE
WHEN WE'RE OUTSIDE

Glen Ogle Viaduct

Whether it's a short walk during our lunch break or a full day's outdoor adventure, we know that a good dose of fresh air is just the tonic we all need.

At Ordnance Survey (OS), we're passionate about helping more people to get outside more often. It sits at the heart of everything we do, and through our products and services, we aim to help you lead an active outdoor lifestyle, so that you can live longer, stay younger and enjoy life more.

We firmly believe the outdoors is for everyone, and we want to help you find the very best Great Britain has to offer. We are blessed with an island that is beautiful and unique, with a rich and varied landscape. There are coastal paths to meander along, woodlands to explore, countryside to roam, and cities to uncover. Our trusted source of inspirational content is bursting with ideas for places to go, things to do and easy beginner's guides on how to get started.

It can be daunting when you're new to something, so we want to bring you the know-how from the people who live and breathe the outdoors. To help guide us, our team of awe-inspiring OS Champions share their favourite places to visit, hints and tips for outdoor adventures, as well as tried and tested accessible, family- and wheelchair-friendly routes. We hope that you will feel inspired to spend more time outside and reap the physical and mental health benefits that the outdoors has to offer. With our handy guides, paper and digital mapping, and exciting new apps, we can be with you every step of the way.

To find out more visit os.uk/getoutside

RESPECTING
THE COUNTRYSIDE

You can't beat getting outside in the Scottish countryside, but it's vital that we leave no trace when we're enjoying the great outdoors.

Let's make sure that generations to come can enjoy the countryside just as we do.

 Care for your environment

 Keep your dog under proper control

 Take responsibility for your own actions

 Respect people's privacy and peace of mind

 Take extra care if organising a group or event

 Help land managers and others to work safely and effectively

For more details please visit
www.outdooraccess-scotland.scot

USING THIS GUIDE

Easy-to-follow Loch Lomond and the Trossachs walks for all

Before setting off

Check the walk information panel to plan your outing

- Consider using **Public transport** where flagged. If driving, note the satnav postcode for the car park under **Parking**
- The suggested **Time** is based on a gentle pace
- Note the availability of **Cafés**, tearooms and pubs, and **Toilets**

Terrain and hilliness

- **Terrain** indicates the nature of the route surface
- Any rises and falls are noted under **Hilliness**

Walking with your dog?

- This panel states where **Dogs** must be on a lead and how many stiles there are – in case you need to lift your dog
- Keep dogs on leads where there are livestock and between April and August in forest and on grassland where there are ground-nesting birds

A perfectly pocket-sized walking guide

- Handily sized for ease of use on each walk
- When not being read, it fits nicely into a pocket...
- ...so between points, put this book in the pocket of your coat, trousers or day sack and enjoy your stroll in glorious national park countryside – we've made it pocket-sized for a reason!

Flexibility of route presentation to suit all readers

- **Not comfortable map reading?** Then use the simple-to-follow route profile and accompanying route description and pictures
- **Happy to map read?** New-look walk mapping makes it easier for you to focus on the route and the points of interest along the way
- Read the insightful **Did you know?**, **Local legend**, **Stories behind the walk** and **Nature notes** to help you make the most of your day out and to enjoy all that each walk has to offer

OS information about the walk

- Many of the features and symbols shown are taken from Ordnance Survey's celebrated **Explorer** mapping, designed to help people across Great Britain enjoy leisure time spent outside

OS information

NS 391822
Explorer OL38

- National Grid reference for the start point
- Explorer sheet map covering the route

The easy-to-use walk map

- **Large-scale** mapping for ultra-clear route finding

- **Numbered points** at key turns along the route that tie in with the route instructions and respective points marked on the profile

- **Pictorial symbols** for intuitive map reading, see Map Symbols on the front cover flap

The simple-to-follow walk profile

- Progress easily along the route using the illustrative profile, it has **numbered points** for key turning points and **graduated distance** markers

- Easy-read **route directions** with turn-by-turn detail

- Reassuring **route photographs** for each numbered point

 Scotland Great
   Trail

3 ► At blue sign, leave Three Lochs Way, turning **right** down steep path that (literally) ducks under railway. ► Behind houses bear **right**, signed Three Villages Hall, and follow signs **left** then **right** to descend beside church to a road.

Using QR codes

• Scan each QR code to see the route in Ordnance Survey's OS Maps App.
NB You may need to download a scanning app if you have an older phone

• OS Maps will open the route automatically if you have it installed. If not, the route will open in the web version of OS Maps

• Please click **Start Route** button to begin navigating or **Download Route** to store the route for offline use

WALK 1

BALLOCH

Balloch Castle Country Park is one of the most popular destinations in the national park – no wonder, as its good paths wind through lovely scenery. Originally a private estate, the designed landscape of ornamental woodlands, open parkland, gardens and tree-lined avenues was developed in the 18th and 19th centuries. Its castle, a gothic-style mansion, is set in a commanding position overlooking Loch Lomond. It's easy to make your visit a day out with nearby attractions within easy walking distance.

OS information	
🧭 NS 391822 Explorer OL38	
Distance 2.7 miles/4.3km	
Time 1½ hours	
Start/Finish Balloch	
Parking G83 8LQ Moss o' Balloch car park, Balloch Road	
Public toilets Castle car park and bus station, 200 yards east of 🧭 car park entrance	
Cafés/pubs Balloch	
Terrain Tarmac paths	
Hilliness Gradual climb to Balloch Castle; steep descent ⑥ to ⑦	
Footwear Year round 🥾	

Public transport

Train services from Glasgow–Balloch Railway Station is 350 yards west of car park entrance at 🚶: scotrail.co.uk; Scottish Citylink bus services – Balloch Bus Station is 200 yards east of car park entrance: citylink.co.uk

♿ Accessibility
●●●●●●●●●●●

Wheelchair and pushchair friendly; the descent **6** to **7** may be too steep for manual wheelchairs

Dogs

Welcome. No stiles

Did you know? The name Balloch has a Gaelic origin and means 'village on the loch'. It lies on the south shore of Loch Lomond, where the River Leven flows out of the loch. Balloch is a major gateway to the national park and has a large VisitScotland information centre. The town is easy to reach, especially from Glasgow and the South, and has frequent bus and train services.

Local legend Historian Hugh McArthur believes that Loch Lomond is the true site of the lake in the legend of King Arthur and that Avalon was on one of its islands. In his book *King Arthur and the Lake: A Secret History of Loch Lomond*, he highlights that nearby Dumbarton Rock means 'Fortress of the Britons' and that Ben Arthur (the Arrochar hill also known as The Cobbler) could be named after the king.

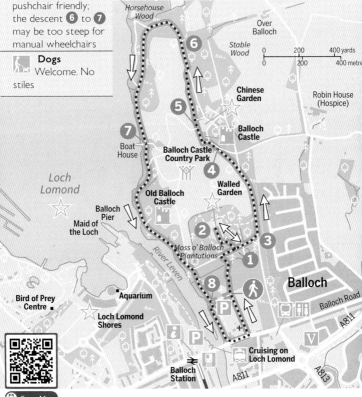

STORIES BEHIND THE WALK

🏛 Balloch Castle Country Park

In 1914, Glasgow Corporation bought the castle and estate as an attraction for people from the city to visit. The 200 acres of parkland and woodland have good paths and lovely views over Loch Lomond. Highlights include ornamental woodlands, a castle-themed Play Park and Walled and Chinese Gardens. It is the only registered historic designed landscape within Loch Lomond and the Trossachs National Park.

🏰 Balloch Castle

Old Balloch Castle was built by the Earls of Lennox in 1238. They were granted the land in 1072 by King Malcolm III, whose father Duncan was murdered by Macbeth. Around 1390 they abandoned the castle for a safer site on Inchmurrin, one of Loch Lomond's islands. All that remains now are traces of a mound and moat, because in 1808 the estate's new owner, John Buchanan of Ardoch, used its stones to build the new Balloch Castle (currently closed).

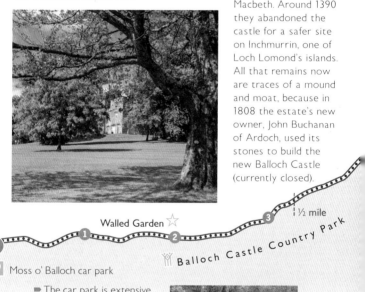

Walled Garden ☆

🚶 ━━━━ ①━━━━━━② ━━━━③ ½ mile

🅿 Moss o' Balloch car park

Balloch Castle Country Park

➤ The car park is extensive. Walk to its far right end and take path signed for Walled Garden and Balloch Castle.
➤ After stream goes under path, turn **right** at T-junction and walk 100 yards to next fingerpost.

☆ Loch Lomond Shores

This attraction across the River Leven offers leisure experiences and shopping. It hosts a department store and a curving arcade of shops and cafés. Drumkinnon Tower is home to a Sea Life Aquarium and offers a superb view up the loch. There is also a Bird of Prey Centre and Tree Zone Aerial Adventure Course. Loch Lomond Shores has its own car park or you can walk to it via the far bank of the River Leven.

🖼 Cruising on Loch Lomond

Sweeney's Cruises operate from the east side of Balloch Bridge (by the visitor information centre). They run 1- and 2-hour cruises that circuit some of Loch Lomond's islands, and provide views of Ben Lomond and a number of Loch Lomond's stately homes and castles along the shoreline. They also operate Waterbus ferry services to other places up the loch. The *Maid of the Loch*, the last paddle-steamer built in the UK, is being restored by volunteers.

Chinese Garden ☆

Balloch Castle 🏰

Balloch Castle Country Park

1 mile

Horsehouse Wood

1 ➤ Turn **left**, signed Walled Garden then go **left** again at Y-junction.
➤ Take first **right** between hedges to an arch into Walled Garden.

2 ➤ After exploring Walled Garden, retrace steps to fingerpost at **1** and turn **left** for Balloch Castle.
➤ Keep **ahead** over a crossroads to a wide triangular junction with grass in middle.

3 ➤ Turn **left** up a broad tarmac path.
➤ Fork **left** where it splits and soon pass metal bollards and join drive up to Balloch Castle.

NATURE NOTES

Balloch Castle Country Park contains many exotic, ornamental trees, planted to enhance the landscape. Both mature and young specimens of monkey puzzle can be seen around ❺. The species comes from the mountains of South America and is so named because climbing the branches of spiked leaves would be a puzzle even for a monkey.

The sweet chestnut is also called the Spanish chestnut, reflecting its origins in a sunnier Mediterranean climate. It produces edible nuts that are traditionally roasted or ground into flour. In Scotland the nuts rarely develop fully.

Yew is used here for hedges; the trees are poisonous and often planted in churchyards to keep out livestock.

Wildflowers such as harebell bloom in the wilder parts where the grass isn't mown.

Mute swans live around the River Leven. They build nests of piled reeds and lay large white eggs that hatch into fluffy grey cygnets. The young remain with the parents until they next breed, when they are chased away to find their own territories.

The small copper butterfly likes warm, dry grassland where it often basks on bare ground.

Balloch Castle Country Park

Boat House ⑦

1½ miles

Old Balloch Castle

❹ ➡ Walk to **left** side of castle and go **right** round its corner.
➡ Enjoy fine views over the parkland and keep **ahead** to a junction (where steps lead to Chinese Garden on right).

❺ ➡ Continue **ahead** (left is a shortcut to Boat House).
➡ When another path joins from the right, **continue** in same direction, initially with hedge on your right, to next junction.

❻ ➡ Keep **left** of map board and stay on main path as it goes downhill and gradually curves 180 degrees left.
➡ Remain on main path and emerge from woods by play area and slipway.

Above: sweet chestnut
Below: yew

Top: harebell
Above: mute swan
Below: monkey
puzzle tree

Cruising on Loch Lomond
(opposite bank of River Leven)

Moss o' Balloch
car park

2½ miles

200 yards right

275 yards left

at bus station

miles

River Leven (right)
Balloch Castle Country Park

7 ➤ Keep **ahead**, signed Balloch, past Boat House and beside loch.
➤ After path curves round old castle earthworks, ignore all left turns and keep **ahead** with the River Leven on your right to another slipway.

8 ➤ Bear **right** after slipway, to keep by river (left is shortcut to car park).
➤ At road bridge, follow path up slope and go **left** on pavement then first **left** into car park.

TAKE A FERRY

INCHCAILLOCH

On this walk you can enjoy the excitement of a boat trip on Loch Lomond and explore one of its many islands. Inchcailloch is a wonderful place to visit because of its rich natural and cultural heritage. Here you can experience remoteness and wildness in a safe and easily accessible location. The summit view stretches up the loch to Ben Lomond. Arrive via a short boat trip from Balmaha on the east shore or a longer cruise from Luss in the west.

OS information

🏃 NS 413906
Explorer OL38

Distance
1.9 miles/3 km

Time
1¼ hours

Start/Finish
North Jetty, Inchcailloch (if arriving at Port Bawn jetty from Luss, start at ⑤)

Parking G63 0JQ
Balmaha Visitor Centre car park, Balmaha
(G83 8PA Luss Visitor Centre car park, Luss)

Public toilets
Balmaha; Luss; compost toilet near ⑤, Port Bawn

Cafés/pubs
None on the island. Nearest at Balmaha or Luss

Terrain
Woodland paths with steps, rocky in places

Hilliness
Moderate climb and descent on Low Path and Central Valley; Summit Path is steeper up and down

Footwear
Winter 👢
Spring/Summer/Autumn 👟

Public transport

Bus stops at Balmaha and Luss car parks: lochlomond-trossachs.org/plan-your-visit/getting-around-the-park/by-bus-or-train. Boat trips from Balmaha Boatyard: balmahaboatyard.co.uk/ferrytoinchcailleoch. Boat trips from Luss Pier: cruiselochlomond.co.uk/luss-inchcailloch-ferry

Did you know? Inchcailloch has a resident population of fallow deer, which are not native to Scotland. They were probably introduced by King Robert the Bruce in the 1300s. In the centuries before wolves were exterminated, the island made a safe deer park where only the king and certain Highland chiefs were allowed to hunt.

Local legend The custom at Highland funerals was for mourners and coffin bearers to be plied with whisky. Often this turned them into drunken affairs where people lost the body or forgot to bury it. In 1645 an edict was passed banning drinking at funerals. This didn't have much effect, so landing bodies on the shore and carrying them up to the burial ground through 'Coffin Valley', the gap between the two hills, would have been a risky business.

Accessibility

Not suitable for wheelchairs; Central Valley Path useable for all-terrain pushchairs

Dogs Welcome but keep under close control between 1 April and 1 July due to ground-nesting birds. No stiles

Scan Me

Walk 2 Inchcailloch 21

STORIES BEHIND THE WALK

☆ **Clashing of continents** Highlands and Lowlands meet on Inchcailloch, with mountainous landscapes to the north and gentler ones to the south. The contrasting landscapes are a result of differing geology. The island lies on the Highland Boundary Fault, a deep fracture in the Earth's crust where two continents collided 450 million years ago, creating a broad crumple zone. You can trace the fault as a ridge that runs down Conic Hill, above Balmaha, and across the neighbouring island of Inchmurrin.

Inchcailloch

A special place for wildlife, Inchcailloch is part of the Loch Lomond National Nature Reserve, which includes the mouth of the River Kendrick, south of Balmaha. The island is cloaked in native woodland, which forms a billowing canopy when viewed from the water. The woodland is composed mainly of oak, which supports more insects, birds and other life forms than any other tree species. Look out for redstarts, wood warblers, woodpeckers and treecreepers, which all nest here.

Central Valley Path (ahead) ①

Exposed rock faces: puddingstone

Summit ②

Summit path

Inchcailloch

North Jetty

➡ From North Jetty, climb steps past National Nature Reserve sign and follow path to map boards and wooden direction sign at path junction.
➡ If landing at Port Bawn Jetty, start from ⑤.

① ➡ Go **left** up Summit Path, (or ahead through Central Valley for easier path to Port Bawn).
➡ Pass smaller hill then climb flights of steps that zigzag up to a bench on the summit of the main hill.

☆ **Glimpse of the past** For many centuries Inchcailloch would have looked very different, as people used to live and farm here. The moss-covered ruin at ❻ is the only trace of the last family to live on the island. They would have grown oats and barley, and kept cattle, sheep and hens. But oak timber became more profitable for the landlord and in 1796 the farmer was asked to plant acorns, turning farmland into woodland.

✛ **A holy place** Inchcailloch means 'island of the old or cowled woman', a name that refers to the Irish missionary, St Kentigerna, who died here in CE 734. She was the daughter of an Irish king and mother of St Fillan, who spread Christianity further through Scotland. Legend is that she established a nunnery on the island. The church built here 500 years later was dedicated to her. The surrounding burial ground has the graves of many clan chiefs, including Rob Roy MacGregor's cousin.

½ mile

S u m m i t   P a t h

Central Valley Path (right) ❸

☆ Clashing of continents

I n c h c a i l l o c h

❹ ✕

❺ ⌂ Port Bawn

❷ ➤ Enjoy wide views before continuing on path over top.
➤ Weave steeply downhill, under some pine trees, to T-junction with wooden sign.

❸ ➤ Join the Central Valley path (right is shortcut back to North Jetty) and go **left** down it to Port Bawn with picnic area behind beach.

NATURE NOTES

The coats of fallow deer vary from pale fawn to dark grey and many have Bambi-like white spots. During the mating season in September, the island rings to the groaning roars of the bucks.

The exposed rock face by post 10 between ① and ② is conglomerate, commonly called puddingstone because the pebbles jutting out of the rock face look like fruit in a pudding. It was laid down more than 400 million years ago when rivers washed sand, silt and pebbles down from ancient mountains in the north.

The dor beetle has a metallic blue sheen and digs burrows for its eggs and larvae, which it feeds with mammal dung. It plays a useful recycling role, turning the droppings of fallow deer, fox and other creatures into new life that birds, badgers and others can feed on.

Dead wood is an important element of woodland ecology. Insects and fungi feed on the rotting timber, gradually breaking it down and returning its nutrients to the soil to sustain new growth.

Bluebells bloom in the oakwoods in May and have succulent strap-like leaves. The more fibrous leaves of woodrush look similar but don't die back, remaining green all winter.

Holly berries are an important winter food for blackbirds and thrushes.

1 mile

L o w   P a t h
I n c h c a i l l o c h

6
☆
Glimpse
the pas

⑤ ➡ From jetty, return along walkway, keep **right** of Welcome to Inchcailloch map and turn **left** between wooden railings.
➡ Walk past compost toilets then bear **right** on Low Path and follow it for ½ mile through oak woodland beside shore to a fork.

④ ➡ Bear **right** beyond Ranger Hut onto walkway leading to Port Bawn Jetty and view over bay.

Above: dor beetle
Top left: fallow deer
Opposite: holly berries

Top right: puddingstone **Above**: dead wood

1½ miles

7

+ A holy place

L o w   P a t h

Junction with
Central Valley Path

I n c h c a i l l o c h

North Jetty

6 ➦ At fork, with post 5, go **left** 20 yards to mossy ruins of old farm (glimpse of the past) then keep **right** of it.
➦ Rejoin main path, which zigzags up steps, then keep **ahead** at sign to visit burial ground and church ruins.

7 ➦ Return to main path, bear **left** down steps to T-junction and turn **left**, signed North Jetty (right through Central Valley is shortcut return to **5**).
➦ At next sign keep **ahead** and go down steps to North Jetty (or turn **right** onto Summit Path if started at **5**).

This page (clockwise): Ben Ledi from Callander;
Luss; Tourist shop, Callander; River Cononish, Tyndrum
Opposite (clockwise): Drumkinnon, Loch Lomond;
Brig o'Turk; sculpture project, Lochearnhead

ROB ROY
HERO or VILLAIN?
Audio & Visual Display Inside >>

WALK 3

CATCH A BUS

LUSS

The conservation village of Luss is a magnet for visitors, who love to wander around its attractive streets, photograph cottages bedecked with flowers and picnic on its long, sandy beach. From the promenade the views across Loch Lomond to Ben Lomond are magnificent. This walk combines three trails – Lochside, River and Quarry paths – for a full circuit of the village and surrounding countryside. Look out for the ancient churchyard and animal carvings in the woods.

OS information

🅭 NS 359930
Explorer OL38

Distance
1.5 miles/2.4km

Time
1 hour

Start/Finish
Luss

Parking G83 8PG
Luss Visitor Centre car park (alternative parking nearby at Luss South car park)

Public toilets
In Visitor Centre car park

Cafés/pubs
Luss

Terrain
Tarmac surfaces on Lochside and Riverside paths then rougher ground and steps on Quarry Path

Hilliness
Level on Lochside and Riverside paths; gradual climb on Quarry Path

Footwear
Winter (for Quarry Path) 🥾
Spring/Summer/Autumn 👟

Public transport

Bus stop in Visitor Centre car park for services 302, Carrick Castle to Helensburgh: garelochheadcoaches.co.uk; and 305, Alexandria to Luss: mccolls.org.uk; bus stop on A82 for Scottish Citylink service Glasgow–Oban: citylink.co.uk

Accessibility

Wheelchair and pushchair friendly to ❸ (keep right at steps) with return to car park along village road pavement

Dogs

Welcome. No stiles

Did you know? At 24 miles long and 5 miles across at its widest point, and known as the 'Queen of Scottish lochs', Loch Lomond is the largest lake in Britain by surface area. It has an average depth of 121 feet, but is 643 feet at its deepest point, north of Tarbet. The southern part has many wooded islands, whose names all begin 'Inch', which comes from the Gaelic 'innes' and means small island.

Local legend Luss was originally called Clachan Dhu (the dark village) because it lay in the shadow of the hills. In CE 510 St Kessog, an Irish missionary, founded a church here and set up a monastery on Inchtavannach, a nearby island. After being martyred his body was embalmed with sweet herbs which, according to legend, grew and covered his grave. This gave a new name to the village – 'lus' is Gaelic for herb.

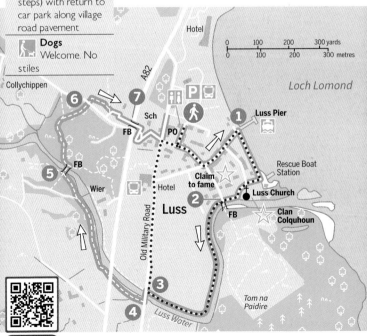

STORIES BEHIND THE WALK

☆ **Claim to fame** At one time, Luss was a hive of industry, with quarries where men hewed slate that went to roof buildings in Glasgow. In 1850 the local laird cleared the workers' old turf-thatched homes and built a new model village for them. Today, the pretty cottages are part of a conservation village. Luss became familiar to many television viewers during the 1980s and 90s as it was used for shooting outdoor scenes for the popular soap *High Road*.

🖼 Luss Pier

Built in 1875 as the village started to become a tourist destination, the pier became a popular place to board boat trips around Loch Lomond. In the second half of the 20th century, the *Maid of the Loch*, the last paddle steamer built in Britain, used to visit daily. Nowadays, the pier is used by companies who offer loch cruises and Waterbus services to other villages.

Claim to fame ☆   Luss Pier 🖼   Clan Colquhoun ☆

 Luss Visitor Centre car park

Promenade Rescue Boat Station   Luss Chu
Loch Lomond

➡ Walk to the village side of the car park and leave it by a lane to the **left** of toilets.
➡ Turn **left** at T-junction and **left** again at crossroads (by Luss General Stores) to reach the pier.

1 ➡ Turn **right** along the promenade and by Rescue Boat Station curve **right** on path.
➡ Pass gate by Luss Church, join lane and go **left** along it round church then beside river towards a footbridge.

† Luss Church The parish church was built in 1875 by Sir James Colquhoun in memory of his father and companions who drowned while returning from a hunting expedition on one of Loch Lomond's islands. Constructed on the site of St Kessog's Church, the graveyard is much older. The earliest stones date from the 7th century and include an 11th-century Viking hogback grave, which can be seen just inside the west gate.

☆ **Clan Colquhoun**

The lands on the west side of Loch Lomond were granted to the Colquhouns in medieval times and the family is still the major landowner around Luss. The Clan motto 'If I Can' dates from the 15th century when the king asked the clan chief to recapture Dumbarton Castle. This was his reply and, after the venture proved successful, it was adopted as part of the clan's coat-of-arms.

Wheelchairs and pushchairs follow path to right for return to car park

L u s s   W a t e r

Footbridge to the Glebe

½ mile

2 ➡ Keep **ahead** past footbridge (or detour over it for loop round the Glebe) and go through wooden gate to left of River Cottage.
➡ Stroll beside Luss Water, gradually curving **right** round field until you come to a high wall.

3 ➡ Climb steps **ahead** to fingerpost (or keep right along level path for shortcut to car park).
➡ Go **left** on Old Military Road (signed Quarry Path) and **cross** bridge over river to another fingerpost on opposite side.

NATURE NOTES

Luss slate quarries were in operation as far back as 1439 and the last one closed in 1955. The slate is part of a belt, about a mile wide, that outcrops along the northern edge of the Highland Boundary Fault. It was formed when clayey sediments were subjected to extreme heat and pressure, creating a strong greyish rock that can be split into thin slabs.

Great spotted woodpeckers live in woodland where they bore nest holes in rotten wood. They can be seen clinging vertically to tree trunks, searching for wood-boring insects and their larvae, as well as spiders. In spring the males produce a drumming sound by hammering on dry branches in the treetops.

The elegant, medium-sized roe deer is a common sight in woods and farmland. Their coats are brown, turning reddish in summer and greyer in winter. The bucks have small antlers. They have no tails and a whitish rump, which is very noticeable when they bound away from danger.

Oak trees provide habitat for more insects, lichen and birds than any other tree species.

The common blue butterfly likes sunny, sheltered places with short vegetation. The orange-tip butterfly favours hedgerow verges.

Honeysuckle climbs up trees and has a sweet scent.

The chanterelle fungus smells of apricots.

Luss Water 1 mile

4 A82 underpass 5 Steps

4 ➤ Go through gate, down steps and cross footbridge over side stream then walk under A82.

➤ Follow rougher path upriver and fork **right** when level with weir, continuing beside wooden fence to footbridge.

5 ➤ Turn **right** to cross footbridge over river then climb steps beside slate quarry spoil heap.

➤ At top keep **ahead** over crossroads onto path with wooden fence on right and follow it through wood to lane.

Roe deer

Top left: common blue
Top middle: chanterelle
Top right: great
spotted woodpecker
Above: slate

A82 footbridge

Steps

1½ miles

Luss Visitor
Centre car park

6 ➡ Walk across road and take path to **right** on far side, passing between wooden barriers and soon reaching kissing-gate.
➡ Go through onto lane and keep **ahead** past big house to footbridge.

7 ➡ Cross the bridge over the A82 and go down steps on the far side (choice of steep or shallow).
➡ Bear **right** to a crossroads and turn **left** back into the car park.

ARROCHAR

Tarbet and Arrochar are only a mile apart, but the former borders freshwater Loch Lomond and the latter fringes the seashore of Loch Long. This walk links them, following the Arrochar Heritage Trail and parts of the Three Lochs Way. The views are impressive, especially over Loch Long to the Arrochar Alps. These mountains played a significant role in the development of Scottish climbing in the late 1800s, thanks to the Cobbler Club, named after the most popular hill.

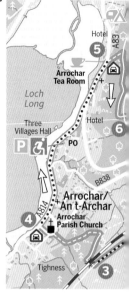

OS information

🚶 NN 311044
Explorer OL39

Distance
4 miles / 6.4 km

Time
2¼ hours

Start/Finish
Arrochar & Tarbet Station

Parking G83 7DB
Roadside parking bays, Station Road, Tarbet (larger car park at Tarbet Pier, ½ mile east of 🚶, G83 7DG)

Public toilets
Tarbet Pier car park

Cafés/pubs
Arrochar; Tarbet

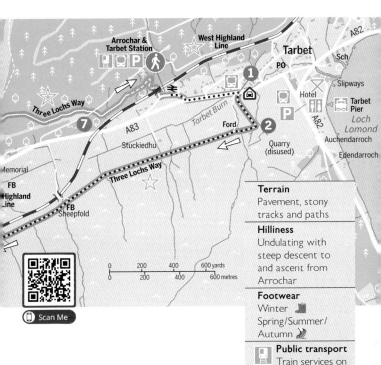

Terrain
Pavement, stony tracks and paths

Hilliness
Undulating with steep descent to and ascent from Arrochar

Footwear
Winter 🥾
Spring/Summer/Autumn 👟

Public transport
Train services on the Glasgow–Oban line: scotrail.co.uk. Scottish Citylink bus services to Tarbet with stops at 🚶, ① and Tarbet Pier car park: citylink.co.uk

Accessibility
Wheelchairs and pushchairs in Arrochar, ④ to ⑤; powered wheelchairs and all-terrain pushchairs 🚶 to ③

Dogs
Welcome. No stiles

Did you know? Torpedoes were tested in Loch Long between 1912 and 1986. The British Admiralty operated from piers and buildings across the loch from Arrochar. The length, straightness and depth of the loch made it ideal as a torpedo firing range. The structures have lain derelict for years and planning permission to incorporate them into a luxury hotel and marina has lapsed.

Local legend The lands around Arrochar belonged to the MacFarlane clan from 1225 to 1785, when they were forced to sell to Sir Malcolm Colquhoun of Luss to pay their debts. The clan became notorious as cattle raiders, stealing cattle from neighbours and hiding them in the mountains near Loch Sloy in the dead of night. Such was their reputation that the local name for the moon used to be 'MacFarlane's lantern'.

STORIES BEHIND THE WALK

☆ **Gaelic names** Arrochar derives from the Gaelic word 'arachor' meaning 'ploughgate'. It is an ancient Scottish measurement of land, equal to 104 acres, and is the area a team of eight oxen could plough in a season. Tarbet comes from the Gaelic 'tairbeart', meaning 'portage', a place where boats could be carried from one body of water to another. The name is shared with many other geographically similar places in Scotland.

☆ **Troubled times** Viking raiders were attracted to the rich farmlands around the west coast of Scotland. In 1263 King Hakon of Norway sent 60 longboats up Loch Long, commanded by Magnus, King of Man. The Vikings dragged their boats across the isthmus to Loch Lomond so they could sail south and attack inland settlements. Later that year the Vikings were defeated at the Battle of Largs (south of Glasgow), but some may have settled in this area.

West Highland Line

Tarbet Pier car park ¼ mile along A83

½ mile

Arrochar and Tarbet Station

☆ Three Lochs Way

➥ With your back to station follow blue Three Lochs Way sign towards Loch Lomond and Tarbet Pier, walking downhill past lay-by.
➥ At T-junction with main road (A83) turn **left** and walk on pavement as far as bus stop.

1 ➥ **Cross** road to tarmac lane opposite, signed for Garelochhead on the Three Lochs Way.
➥ Go through gate at bottom and climb uphill, gaining a view of Loch Lomond, to junction.

☆ **West Highland Line** Arrochar & Tarbet Station is on the West Highland Line, one of the most scenic train journeys in the world. The line took seven years to build and opened in 1894. It was not without cost, as 37 navvies died while constructing this stretch of the line. They were buried in the graveyard of Ballyhennan Church, which is now The Slanj bar and restaurant.

☆ **Three Lochs Way** This long-distance trail starts in Balloch at the south end of Loch Lomond, crosses hills to Helensburgh on Gare Loch then runs above Loch Long before finishing further north up Loch Lomond at Inveruglas. The 34-mile route takes the walker from Lowland to Highland scenery. It can be completed in three to four days, but also lends itself to day walks.

☆ **Three Lochs Way**

2 ➟ Turn first **right** and go through Luss Estates gate with view over Tarbet.
➟ Walk along undulating gravel track for nearly 1¼ miles (old sheepfold is almost hidden on right half-way along) to path signed Arrochar.

3 ➟ At blue sign, leave Three Lochs Way, turning **right** down steep path that (literally) ducks under railway.
➟ Behind houses bear **right**, signed Three Villages Hall, and follow signs **left** then **right** to descend beside church to a road.

NATURE NOTES

Maidenhair spleenwort is a small delicate fern that grows in crevices between rocks, on mossy branches and in walls, including on the old sheepfold midway between ❷ and ❸. The short, round leaflets run in pairs up a central black stem. It spreads by means of spores, released from the underside of its leaves.

The tall, branched marsh thistle has purple flowers. It likes wet ground, but can also grow in drier rough places. Its flowers are a valuable nectar source for butterflies and other insects.

Spangle galls are little disks that form on the underside of oak leaves. Each contains the larva of a tiny wasp. In autumn the galls fall from the leaves and carpet the ground. Most are covered by leaf litter, which protects the developing larvae that emerge in April.

The hazel is a small deciduous tree with rounded leaves. It produces dangling catkins in spring and nuts in autumn.

Top: maidenhair spleenwort
Above: spangle galls

Arrochar Parish
✝ Church

Three Villages Hall
(information boards)

Arrochar
Tea Room

3 mi

2 miles

❹

P

2½ miles

❺ 🔲 Steps

Loch Long (left)

❺ ➡ Opposite Arrochar Tea Room turn **right** at Three Lochs Way sign, up a path with stone steps.
➡ At junction bear **right**, signed Tairbeirt Station, and keep following yellow-ringed posts to path T-junction.

❹ ➡ Turn **right** along the A814; **cross** the road to use pavement beside Loch Long.
➡ Where road meets A83 keep **ahead** beside loch to Arrochar Tea Room.

The small pearl-bordered fritillary has silvery spots on its underwings, while the upper sides are chequered in orange and black.

Bracken is a large, coarse fern that is widespread in woodland and on hillsides.

Puffball fungi grow in grassland and when ripe release a dust-like cloud of spores.

Above: puffball fungi
Below: marsh thistle

small pearl-bordered fritillary butterfly

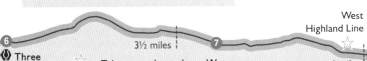

West Highland Line

6
Three Lochs Way   3½ miles   **7**   Three Lochs Way   4 miles
Arrochar & Tarbet Station

6 ➡ Turn **right**, briefly downhill, before climbing with views then descending through trees.
➡ Pass between wooden barriers to forest road.

7 ➡ Go diagonally across forest road and down path on far side into lovely oak woodland.
➡ After ¼ mile, at path junction, bend sharp **right** downhill, past wooden barriers and through railway underpass, back to start.

Opposite (clockwise): orange-tip
butterfly; Highland cow; hard fern; ash
This page (clockwise): small tortoiseshell
butterfly; birch trees; oak coppice

40

TYNDRUM

In medieval times, there would have been as many people living around the tiny hamlet of Dalrigh as in Tyndrum, the village to the north. While Dalrigh became a backwater, Tyndrum, at a junction of roads through the Highlands, developed into a busy stopping place for travellers. Its growth was aided by the arrival of the railways, with two stations on the West Highland Line: the Lower on the Oban branch, and the Upper on the Fort William branch, both very scenic routes.

OS information

☆ NN 343 291
Explorer OL39

Distance
3.6 miles/5.7 km

Time
2 hours

Start/Finish
Dalrigh

Parking FK20 8RX
Tyndrum Community Woodland car park, Dalrigh

Public toilets
Tyndrum, on A82 between ② and ③

Cafés/pubs
Tyndrum

Terrain
Tarmac cycle path; gravel tracks; narrow paths with muddy patches

Hilliness
Gently undulating

Did you know? Dalrigh and Tyndrum lie in Strathfillan, a valley that was a busy thoroughfare long before trains and motor vehicles were invented. Drochaid Bhàn, the stone bridge across the River Fillan at ⑦, is on the Old Military Road from Stirling to Fort William, built in 1748-53 by Major Caulfield. The road allowed the government to move troops around quickly, in order to keep unruly Highlanders under control.

Local legend Near Tyndrum a stream tumbles down the Eas na h-uruisg, which translates as 'urisk's waterfall'. In folklore urisks were hobgoblins who spent their summers among remote Highland streams and came down in winter to shelter in homes and farmhouses. In return for warmth they would perform chores and farming tasks while the inhabitants slept, especially milking the cows, churning butter and cleaning. If upset, they could be mischievous.

Footwear
Winter 🥾
Spring/Summer/
Autumn 👟

Public transport
Scottish Citylink bus services to Tyndrum with bus stop near ③: citylink.co.uk;
Tyndrum has two railway stations – Lower Station, Oban line, and Upper Station, Fort William line: scotrail.co.uk

Accessibility
Cycle path is wheelchair and pushchair friendly, 🚶 to ①, and in Tyndrum

Dogs
Welcome. No stiles

STORIES BEHIND THE WALK

☆ **Battle of Dalrigh** In 1306, Robert the Bruce was defeated in battle near Perth and retreated north with the remains of his army. While camping at Dalrigh, Bruce was ambushed by John of Argyll, chief of the Clan MacDougall. The attack was revenge for Bruce's murder of John Comyn, his rival for the throne of Scotland, who was the clan chief's nephew. Afterwards Bruce went into hiding for two years before returning to rule Scotland. Dalrigh is Gaelic for the 'King's Field'.

☆ **Lochan of the Lost Sword**

The legend is that after defeat at the Battle of Dalrigh, Bruce and his followers threw their claymores (heavy broad swords) into this small loch so they didn't impede their escape. However, the story may be attached to the wrong place. Lochan nan Arm, on the other side of the river, may be a likelier spot as its name means 'small loch of the weapons'.

Tyndrum Community Woodland

↟ ½ mile

🚶 **Tyndrum Community Woodland car park**
🅿

Crianlarich–Tyndrum Cycle Path

➥ From the car park entrance, go **straight across** Dalrigh Road onto the cycle path, signed Crianlarich to Tyndrum.

➥ Stay on this tarmac path for nearly 1 mile, going through three gates and crossing a bridge to reach a T-junction.

1 ➥ Turn **right** on undulating path beside the river.

➥ Go **right** (signed Tyndrum) on meeting road by white cottages.

➥ At T-junction with A82, turn **left** for mid-walk refreshment: Real Food Café, TJ's Diner, The Tyndrum Inn.

⭐ Gold in the hills

Quartz veins running through the hills here are rich in mineral ores. Lead and silver mining are recorded as far back as 1424. Lead began to be commercially exploited in 1741 by Sir Robert Clifton, who extracted many tons, much of it used for gunshot and cannon balls. The lost township of Newtown housed workers for the lead smelter. In 2016, the Cononish gold mine opened and tracks were improved to take mine vehicles, which you may encounter.

🐦 Tyndrum Community Woodland

In 2006, Strathfillan Community Development Trust purchased Tyndrum Community Woodland from the then Forestry Commission. It is mixed woodland, with downy birch, Scots pine, willow and other native species, and includes areas of bog, rough grazing and patches of old spruce plantation. The West Highland Way runs through the area.

🏴 West Highland Way

```
  ↤ 1 mile          Lower Station        Tyndrum   ↦ 1½ miles       Lower Station
                    (Oban Line)        🍽 The Tyndrum Inn          (Oban Line)
                    225 yards left     ☕ TJ's Diner, Real          225 yards ahead
                                          Food Café
```

3 ➡ Turn **right** along Lower Station Road then **left** beyond Bridge Cottage to return to **1**.
➡ Keep **right** across open area, through gate and continue **ahead** on West Highland Way for ¾ mile, passing Lochan of the Lost Sword shortly before reaching T-junction.

2 ➡ Retrace yours steps along main road from Real Food Café, past public toilets, to first junction by big red sign for MGM Hotels.

NATURE NOTES

Red deer are Britain's largest wild land mammal. The stags grow branched antlers each year and use them to fight other males during the autumn breeding season, known as the rut. They can destroy young trees, so high fences are erected to keep them out of newly planted woodlands.

Scotland's moorlands are lit up by bell heather in summer. The deep magenta, bell-shaped flowers attract bees and other pollinators. The plant forms large cushions often growing among the more widespread common heather, which has smaller, paler flowers.

The Scots pine is Britain's only native coniferous tree. It likes dry, often rocky ground and is able to withstand harsh weather. It has an orange-brown scaly bark and blue-green needles that are attached in pairs. The cones contain seeds loved by red squirrels and Scottish crossbills.

Bog myrtle is an aromatic shrub that grows in marshy places and is famous for repelling midges. It is deciduous and turns golden in autumn.

The grey heron stalks the edges of rivers and lochs, waiting to spear a fish or frog with its long beak.

Funnel mushrooms start with domed caps that develop into a funnel-shape as they mature.

Green-veined white butterflies are attracted to damp places in rough grassland.

Lochan of the
Lost Sword ☆

2 miles

2½ miles

Tyndrum Community Woodland

Gold in the h
(200 yards ri

4 ➡ To see the site of Newtown mining village (gold in the hills), detour **right** 200 yards to information board.
➡ But route continues **left** for 250 yards to a fork in the track.

5 ➡ Bear **left** off main track, soon crossing wooden bridge with a 2T sign.
➡ At fork, go **right** on path with thistle marker post to rejoin main track.
➡ Go **right** downhill towards bridge (left is shortcut back to 🅰).

Red deer

Bell heather

Above: grey heron
Below: bog myrtle

Battle of Dalrigh ☆ **(◊) West Highland Way**

Crianlarich-Tyndrum Cycle Path

3 miles

River Cononish

3½ miles

Tyndrum Community Woodland car park

6 ▪ Before bridge, walk **ahead** between rocks and go **left** along West Highland Way beside River Cononish
▪ Walk downstream past the site of the Battle of Dalrigh to a T-junction by an old stone bridge.

7 ▪ Turn **left**, leaving West Highland Way for the Crianlarich to Tyndrum Cycle Path.
▪ Follow tarmac strip of old main road back to car park, going through a gate just before it.

KILLIN

Killin lies at the heart of the historic
region of Breadalbane, the 'High
Country of Alba', the ancient kingdom
of Scotland. The name is appropriate as
the village is surrounded by mountain
ranges, with the Tarmachan ridge
providing a prominent backdrop. The
Falls of Dochart are a memorable sight,
cascading over rocky ledges and under
the old stone bridge. The Dochart is
joined by the River Lochay, another
powerful river, shortly before flowing
into Loch Tay.

OS information
🏃 NN 574332   Explorer OL48
Distance   3.4 miles/5.5km
Time   2 hours
Start/Finish   Killin
Parking FK21 8TE   Car park off Lyon   Road, Killin
Public toilets   In car park
Cafés/pubs   Killin
Terrain   Tarmac pavement   and lanes; paths and   tracks with hardcore   surface but some   prone to mud
Hilliness   Mostly flat, except   for slope up to   Finlarig Castle
Footwear   Winter 🥾   Spring/Summer/   Autumn 👟
Public   **transport**   Bus services to   Killin from: Crieff,   890; Aberfeldy, 893;   Callander, C60; and   on the Stirling–   Tyndrum route, S60:   travelinescotland.com

Did you know? Killin is home to the Healing Stones of St Fillan, who was a notable healer and gave this set of river stones the power to cure illness. Fillan came to Scotland from Ireland in 717 with his mother St Kentigerna (see Walk 2) and was the abbot of a monastery in Fife before retiring to Glen Dochart. Each stone cured a specific part of the body when rubbed over the afflicted area.

Local legend According to local legend, Fingal, the mythical hero of the Ossian saga, is buried in Killin. A standing stone in Breadalbane Park, behind the McLaren Hall, is called Fingal's Stone. Fionn mac Cumhaill (pronounced 'Finn Macool' and modified to 'Fingal') was the leader of a band of warrior heroes who had many adventures around Scotland, aided by his faithful hunting dog Bran.

Accessibility
Wheelchairs and pushchairs throughout but using alternative route along Pier Road to bypass ① – ③

Dogs
Welcome. No stiles

Scan Me

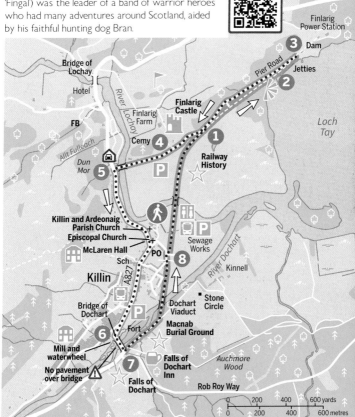

STORIES BEHIND THE WALK

☆ **Macnab Burial Ground** The River Dochart divides under the bridge and flows around Innis Buidhe, the 'Yellow Island', which is the ancient burial ground of the Macnab chiefs. The Macnabs were the dominant clan in this area and Kinnell House was their seat, but they lost power to the Campbells of Breadalbane. The gate onto the island is locked, but the key is available locally (see sign on gate).

☆ **Railway history** In 1886, the Killin branch line of the Callander to Oban railway opened. The station stood where the car park is now and the railway extended another mile north to Loch Tay Station. Here passengers and cargo could transfer to steamboats that sailed the length of Loch Tay. The disused line is now a path and this walk follows it across two railway bridges, including the 37-foot-high Dochart Viaduct, which has five arches.

Wheelchairs/pushchairs use Pier Road, **①**-**③**

Railway history ☆   Loch Tay

River Lochay

① 1½ mile

Car park off Lyon Road

K i l l i n b r a n c h l i n e

P

① ➡ Walk past bus shelter to gap in fence and turn **left** – signposted Loch Tay.
➡ Cross bridge over River Lochay and keep ahead on disused railway line until the access onto Pier Road, opposite a gate.

① ➡ Continue **ahead**, parallel to Pier Road on same path, which can be muddy (wheelchairs follow road).
➡ For view down Loch Tay, go through next gate on **right** (stepping over stream) and walk 100 yards along path to shore.

Finlarig Castle

Built in the 1400s, the castle was acquired by the Campbells of Breadalbane in 1503 as the clan expanded eastwards, and then was extended in 1609. Chiefs traditionally administered the law locally and you can still see the beheading pit used to execute noble criminals. Common criminals were dispatched from the Hanging Tree. The Campbells moved out of Finlarig after building grander Taymouth Castle at the other end of Loch Tay and Finlarig fell into ruin.

✠ ⊞ Killin heritage Killin has two churches: Killin and Ardeonaig Parish Church, with a 'birdcage' belfry, built in 1744; and the smaller, corrugated-iron, Episcopal Church. The latter was nicknamed 'The Grouse Church', as it was often used by guests attending the Earl of Breadalbane's private shooting parties. Opposite is the McLaren Hall, built in 1935 of concrete that has been shaped to look like blocks of stone. Tweed used to be woven in the mill by the bridge, which has a well-preserved waterwheel.

Finlarig Castle

1 mile   P i e r   R o a d   1½ miles

➤ Return to disused railway path, walking past bollards and beside loch until you reach gates into private houses.
➤ Turn 180 degrees **left** onto Pier Road.

3 ➤ Walk along Pier Road, past accesses to **2** and **1**, until the lane forks.
➤ Go **right** a few paces towards sign for Finlarig House, Cottage and Farm.

4 ➤ Turn **right** again up a steep path to Finlarig Castle.
➤ After exploring (stay out of ruins), return to Pier Road and continue past cemetery to T-junction.

NATURE NOTES

Maple trees are planted, as around the car park at 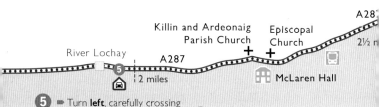, for their ornamental foliage. The leaves emerge red-tinged in spring then become green during the summer. In autumn they change to blazing yellow and red.

One of our tallest, most elegant trees, ash often lines fields and roads. Its leaves have multiple leaflets in opposite pairs along the stem. Many ash trees are suffering from an air-borne fungal disease, ash dieback, and are slowly dying.

Yellow rattle is so called because when its seed pods are ripe you can hear the seeds rattling inside. It is an important component of wildflower meadows, because it is parasitic on grass roots. Its presence reduces the lushness of grasses, allowing more space and light for other wildflowers.

The boletus family of mushrooms includes the 'penny bun', so called because of its appearance. The species has pores rather than gills on the underside of the cap.

Mallard are common on rivers and lochs. The males have bold plumage while the female ducks are a more subtle brown.

The peacock butterfly lays its eggs on nettles and lives for nearly a year after hatching.

River Lochay · A287 · 2 miles

Killin and Ardeonaig Parish Church · Episcopal Church · A287 · 2½ m

McLaren Hall · A28

5 ➤ Turn **left**, carefully crossing the main road to pavement on far side.
➤ Stay on Main Street through centre of village until road bends over Bridge of Dochart (detour **ahead** 30 yards to see old mill and its waterwheel).

6 ➤ Route continues across bridge (take care, no pavement) over Falls of Dochart with Macnab Burial Ground on left.
➤ In front of Falls of Dochart Inn, turn **left** onto track with pillars and Kinnell Estate sign.

Peacock butterfly

Top: penny bun
Middle: maple
Bottom: mallard

Mill and waterwheel (right, 30 yards)

No pavement over bridge

Macnab Burial Ground

River Lochay; Dochart Viaduct

6

7

8

Bridge of Dochart; Falls of Dochart (right)

Falls of Dochart Inn

3 miles

Killin branch line

3½ miles

Car park off Lyon Road

7 ➥ Walk along track and beyond houses fork **left** up ramp onto disused railway line, soon crossing Dochart Viaduct.
➥ Join road and walk **right** for 40 yards to footpath sign by sewage works entrance.

8 ➥ Take path signed Loch Tay, continuing on disused railway back to car park.

KINGSHOUSE TO LOCHEARNHEAD

This walk follows part of a scenic cycle path that winds through native woodland and majestic mountains from Kingshouse to Lochearnhead. Kingshouse is situated at the junction of the A84 and the road to Balquhidder. Lochearnhead is a small village on the western end of Loch Earn at the foot of dramatic Glen Ogle, Scotland's 'Khyber Pass'. You can arrive and depart by bus or park in Lochearnhead and catch the C60 service to Kingshouse, a 5-minute ride.

OS information

NN 564204
Explorer OL46

Distance
3.6 miles/5.7km

Time
2 hours

Start Kingshouse (at bus stop on A84/ Balquhidder road junction)

Finish
Lochearnhead

Parking FK19 8QG Lochearnhead car park, Auchraw Terrace, Lochearnhead

Public toilets
In car park

Cafés/pubs
Kingshouse, Mhor 84; Balquhidder Station, Golden Larches; Lochearnhead, Clachan Cottage Hotel and Lochearnhead Hotel

Terrain
Well-surfaced, dual-purpose cycleway/ footpath

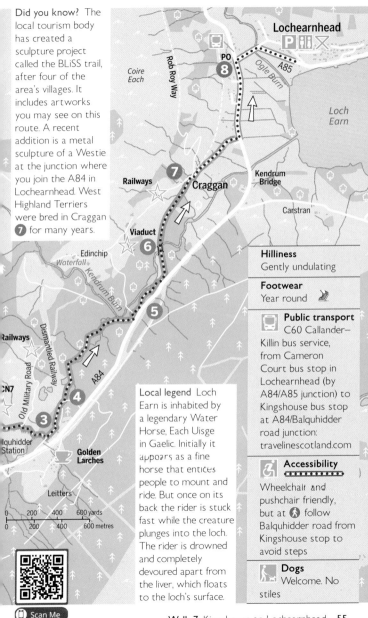

Did you know? The local tourism body has created a sculpture project called the BLiSS trail, after four of the area's villages. It includes artworks you may see on this route. A recent addition is a metal sculpture of a Westie at the junction where you join the A84 in Lochearnhead. West Highland Terriers were bred in Craggan **7** for many years.

Local legend Loch Earn is inhabited by a legendary Water Horse, Each Uisge in Gaelic. Initially it appears as a fine horse that entices people to mount and ride. But once on its back the rider is stuck fast while the creature plunges into the loch. The rider is drowned and completely devoured apart from the liver, which floats to the loch's surface.

Hilliness
Gently undulating

Footwear
Year round

Public transport
C60 Callander–Killin bus service, from Cameron Court bus stop in Lochearnhead (by A84/A85 junction) to Kingshouse bus stop at A84/Balquhidder road junction: travelinescotland.com

Accessibility
Wheelchair and pushchair friendly, but at ☗ follow Balquhidder road from Kingshouse stop to avoid steps

Dogs
Welcome. No stiles

STORIES BEHIND THE WALK

☆ **Rob Roy MacGregor** This walk is along part of the Rob Roy Way, named after the outlaw and Scottish hero, Rob Roy

MacGregor, whose story was romanticised by Sir Walter Scott. He was born on Loch Katrine (site of the clan graveyard) and gained fame as a cattle rustler. On several occasions he escaped custody and likely execution, eventually dying peacefully aged 63 at home in Inverlochlarig. He is buried at Balquhidder, near the start of this walk.

Kingshouse;   Rob Roy
Mhor 84   MacGregor

☆ **Kingshouse**
The Kingshouse Hotel originates from 1590 and was once used by Stewart kings as a royal hunting lodge. It is now the Mhor 84 motel, which serves food and drinks all day. It is part of the Mhor family, which includes Monachyle Mhor, a boutique lochside hotel on Loch Voil beyond Balquhidder. Kingshouse lies on the Old Military Road, built in 1748 by Major Caulfield between Stirling and Fort William.

♦ Rob Roy Way   ½ mile   Balquhidder
                                        Station (right)

☆ National Cycle Network 7

Kingshouse bus stop

➥ To reach Cameron Court bus stop from Lochearnhead car park, turn **right** out of car park and follow A85 pavement ⅓ mile to A84 junction, where the stop is just to the **right**.
➥ Catch bus to Kingshouse.

➥ Go down steps from Kingshouse bus stop to Balquidder road and turn **right** (Mhor 84 is left).
➥ Wheelchairs take road signed Kingshouse and turn **right** onto Balquhidder road.

☆ Railways

On this walk you will follow the course of two branch lines, which met at Balquhidder Station, now a caravan site. The first, from Callander to Oban, was built in 1870. It ran above Lochearnhead and continued to Glen Ogle, crossing an impressive viaduct. The lower line, which curved through Lochearnhead to run along Loch Earn to Crieff, was completed in 1905. They closed in 1965 under the Beeching Plan that cut rural lines from the network.

☆ NCN7

National Cycle Network route 7 runs from Sunderland to Inverness. In Scotland it is known as the 'Lochs and Glens' route. Sustrans, the charity that makes it easier for people to walk and cycle, developed the route using sections of tracks, old railways and purpose-built paths. The biggest challenge on this section was to restore the viaduct over Kendrum Burn. A donation in memory of a cyclist killed on the road funded the bridge that completed the link.

Golden Larches (150 yards, right) ☕

☆ Railways   ☆ National Cycle Network 7

1 mile

① ➤ Immediately beyond A84 underpass, turn **right** onto NCN7, signed Lochearnhead.
➤ Path runs for almost ¾ mile to path junction, initially parallel to road then goes deeper into trees.

② ➤ At junction, ignore small path that goes right to Balquhidder Station (now a caravan park).
➤ Path crosses a stream and in ⅓ mile reaches a T-junction, having curved round a hill with views over native woodland.

1½ miles

③ ➤ At T-junction with tarmac lane, go **left** past a large white house (Golden Larches café is 150 yards right).
➤ Turn next **left** onto broad gravel track and continue to fork.

NATURE NOTES

Beavers are present in this area, having spread from the rivers Tay and Earn, where captive beavers originally escaped into the wild. They are a native species that was exterminated a few centuries ago. Their dams may cause flooding, as occurs on this cycle path, but that can be managed by installing pipes to control the level of their ponds.

The dark green fritillary is a large, strong-flying butterfly that frequents bracken slopes, woodland clearings and rough grassland. The undersides of its orange and black wings have large white spots in a wash of green.

Birch trees are pioneers; their seed spreads on the wind and readily germinates to produce young saplings. Male catkins produce pollen that fertilises the female catkins, which when ripe release masses of seeds. In autumn, the trees light up woods and hillsides with their pale gold foliage.

Canada geese, a non-native species, are now widespread in the wild.

Birch polypore is a bracket fungus that develops a 'hoof' shape as it matures.

The evergreen hard fern produces spores from tall, thin fronds growing out of its centre.

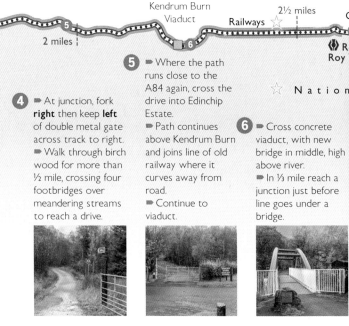

Kendrum Burn Viaduct

Railways

2½ miles

2 miles

5 ➤ Where the path runs close to the A84 again, cross the drive into Edinchip Estate.
➤ Path continues above Kendrum Burn and joins line of old railway where it curves away from road.
➤ Continue to viaduct.

4 ➤ At junction, fork **right** then keep **left** of double metal gate across track to right.
➤ Walk through birch wood for more than ½ mile, crossing four footbridges over meandering streams to reach a drive.

Natio

6 ➤ Cross concrete viaduct, with new bridge in middle, high above river.
➤ In ⅓ mile reach a junction just before line goes under a bridge.

Ro
Roy

Above: dark green fritillary butterfly
Below: birch polypore

Beaver (top) and one of their dams on
the cycle path (bottom)

St Angus Episcopal Church;
A84 junction

A84

Ogle Burn A85

cle   Network 7

3 miles

Cameron Court
bus stop
(65 yards along A84)

3½ miles
Lochearnhead
car park
Loch Earn
(right)

7 ➤ Bear **right**, signed
Lochearnhead, up a ramp and
through a gate into Craggan.
➤ Keep **ahead** down lane to
T-junction with A84 and turn
left on pavement for just
over ¼ mile to A85 junction.

8 ➤ Bus stops are by Cameron
Court, just beyond junction.
➤ To return to car park
turn **right**, signed Perth and
Crieff, and follow road for
⅓ mile, using footbridge
beside narrow road bridge.

THE SLANJ
LOCH LOMOND

BAR
SHOP
RESTAURANT
TEL: 01301 702172

RES AURANT

FALLS OF DOCHART
INN

FALLS OF DOCHART SMOKEHOUS
& SCOTTISH TASTING COUNTE

VILLAGE SHOP

Opposite (clockwise):
Real Food Café,
Tyndrum; Byre Inn,
Brig o'Turk
This page (clockwise):
The Slanj, Arrochar;
Falls of Dochart Inn,
Killin; Village Shop,
Luss; Artisan Café
& Deli, Tyndrum;
Waterhouse Inn,
Balloch

GELATO GIFTS
ICE CREAM

Porrelli

Low Ice Crea

TIGH AN UISGE

Waterhouse Inn

TIG

wine   spirits

THURSE
10.00

HOME M
SCOTTISH S

40

THREE BRIDGES OF CALLANDER

Callander is a bustling tourist town situated on the edge of the Highlands, west of Stirling, where tranquil water meadows meet wooded crags at the foot of the mountains. It has a rich history and numerous cafés, restaurants, shops and hotels. This walk crosses three rivers, the Teith, which flows through the town, and its tributaries, the Eas Gobhain and the Garbh Uisge. The latter flows out of the narrow pass leading north and tumbling over the Falls of Leny.

OS information

🚶 NN 626 079
Explorer OL46

Distance
4.6 miles/7.3km

Time
2½ hours

Start/Finish
Callander

Parking FK17 8BA
Callander Meadows
car park, Leny Road

Public toilets
Station Road car
park, Callander (on
opposite side of A84)

Cafés/pubs
Callander; Trossachs
Woollen Mill café and
Lade Inn, Kilmahog

Terrain
Tarmac and gravel
paths; lanes

Scan Me

Did you know? The sundial at **2** was carved
from limestone in 1733. It stood in the grounds of
a house called Roman Camp, which is now a hotel.
The property belonged to the 2nd Viscount Esher,
a politician with royal connections, who helped
to edit Queen Victoria's papers after her death.
He encouraged local young men to enlist during
World War I and afterwards donated the sundial
to the town.

Local legends The rock on the skyline above **7**
is Samson's Putting Stone, reputed to have been
thrown here by a giant of that name. Geologists
would tell you a different story – that it's an
erratic boulder, carried here by a glacier and left
behind when the thick ice sheet retreated, some
10,000 years ago. As with the neighbouring
hillfort, it's a fine viewpoint reached by detouring
up a steep path.

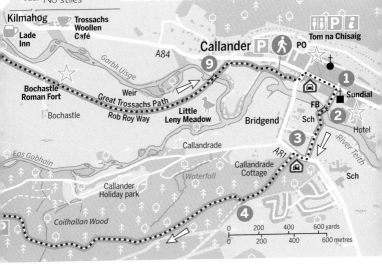

STORIES BEHIND
THE WALK

☆ **Tom na Chisaig** The steep, grassy mound at the start of the walk in named after St Kessog, a major figure in the early Celtic church (see Walk 3). Although he preached in this district, historians believe the mound was built long after his death and is a 'motte' or medieval castle hill. The walled graveyard behind it has an eight-sided watch-house to guard against grave robbers.

☆ **Dunmore Hillfort** The prominent hill above ⑥ is crowned by an Iron Age fort, surrounded by rings of well-preserved ramparts of turf-covered stone. Recent excavation confirmed that Dunmore, which means 'big fort', was occupied in the early to mid-7th century. From the top, extensive views stretch west over Loch Venachar, east to the Pass of Leny and south over the Lowlands.

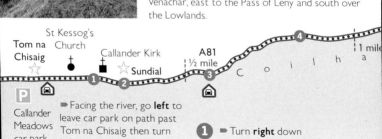

⇒ Facing the river, go **left** to leave car park on path past Tom na Chisaig then turn **left** at road.

⇒ At crossroads turn **right** along Main Street and pass tall spire of St Kessog's Church to next crossroads.

① ⇒ Turn **right** down South Church Street past Callander Kirk.

⇒ Where road ends, keep ahead past historic sundial to River Teith.

☆ Bochastle Roman Fort

Occupied in the CE 80s, this fort still has some upstanding earthworks, which would have been topped by a timber palisade. At that time, the northern frontier of the Roman Empire stretched along the Highland edge and was defended by a chain of forts. These 'glen-blocker' forts controlled trade and defended the occupied Lowlands against attack by Pictish tribes from the Highlands.

Little Leny Meadow

Shortly before **9** an information board marks a path leading across a wet hay meadow that lies on the floodplain between the Teith's two tributaries. This unspoilt grassland is rich in wildflowers, birds and mammals. A stroll across it leads to a medieval chapel and graveyard. This is the burial place of the Buchanans of Leny, including the bard Dugald Buchanan, who helped translate the Bible into Gaelic.

1½ miles

a n W o o d

P

5

Gartchonzie Bridge

2 miles   Eas Gobhain

➡ **Cross** footbridge then turn **left** and stay on tarmac path as it bends **right** up to lane.
➡ Go **straight across** and steeply uphill to road then **right** on pavement for 100 yards.

3 ➡ Turn **left** between pillars onto gravel path into Coilhallan Wood.
➡ Walk uphill for ¼ mile to fingerpost.

4 ➡ Turn **right**, signed Coilhallan Woods car park, soon curving **left** along track.
➡ After 1 mile reach car park and follow exit to road.

NATURE NOTES

Goosanders are normally wary of people, but at Callander Meadows they come close to the riverbank as do other ducks. The females have chestnut heads, while those of males are black with a green sheen. Their long serrated bills help them to catch fish, which is their main source of food.

Having the longest body of any of Britain's species, the golden-ringed dragonfly is a voracious predator. It breeds around acidic streams in moorland and heathland but, being a strong flier, it ranges widely while hunting other dragonflies, wasps, beetles and bumblebees.

Butterfly orchids have grown scarce as their heath and grassland habitats have been drained and improved for grazing. The seedlings rely on a symbiotic fungus for their early development and that is easily killed by fertilisers and fungicides.

Loch Venachar lies between Callander and Brig o'Turk and can be viewed from Dunmore, the Great Trossachs Path or A821 lay-bys.

In autumn water vapour rises from the rivers and lochs around Callander, wreathing Coilhallan Wood in mist.

Larch trees are deciduous conifers that add colour to forests with bright green needles opening in spring and turning golden in autumn.

Common dog violets flower from April to June and may be found across woodland, grassland and heathland habitats. Dog violets are unscented, and this distinguishes them from the fragrant sweet violet.

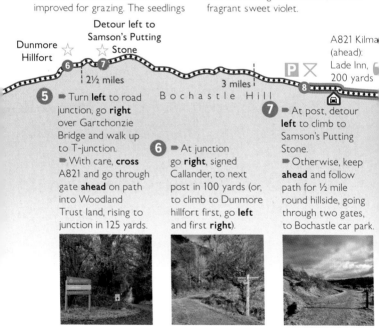

Detour left to
Samson's Putting
☆   ☆ Stone

Dunmore
Hillfort

A821 Kilma⋯ (ahead): Lade Inn, 200 yards

6 ⋯ **7**

2½ miles

3 miles

Bochastle Hill

8

5 ➦ Turn **left** to road junction, go **right** over Gartchonzie Bridge and walk up to T-junction.
➦ With care, **cross** A821 and go through gate **ahead** on path into Woodland Trust land, rising to junction in 125 yards.

6 ➦ At junction go **right**, signed Callander, to next post in 100 yards (or, to climb to Dunmore hillfort first, go **left** and first **right**).

7 ➦ At post, detour **left** to climb to Samson's Putting Stone.
➦ Otherwise, keep **ahead** and follow path for ½ mile round hillside, going through two gates, to Bochastle car park.

Top left: golden-
ringed dragonfly
Above: butterfly orchid
Left: goosanders
Below: dog violet

Bochastle
Roman Fort ☆

Little Leny Meadow

Garb Uisge
Bridge

4½ miles

3½ miles

4 miles

9

Callander
Meadows
car park

P

🐾 **Rob Roy Way;
Great Trossachs Path**

8 ➤ By fingerpost turn sharp
right down tarmac path,
curve down to road and
cross over to cycle path.
➤ Keep **ahead** under bridge
and follow disused railway for
1 mile to the river crossing.

9 ➤ **Cross** metal bridge
over river and keep **ahead**
to signpost.
➤ Go **right** and immediately
left on path back to car park.

BRIG O'TURK

The place name Brig o'Turk means 'Bridge of the Wild Boar' and it's not hard to imagine that the creatures were once hunted in the rugged and intricate landscapes around here. Starting from the Glen Finglas Gateway Centre, where you can learn more about the area, the walk explores local woods, meadows and river. It crosses a wetland called The Mires by a long stretch of boardwalk. Rich in dragonflies and other wildlife, this was once the village curling pond.

OS information

🚶 NN 545065
Explorer OL46

Distance
2.2 miles/3.5km

Time
1¼ hours

Start/Finish
Glen Finglas Gateway Centre, Brig o'Turk

Parking FK17 8HR
Lendrick Hill car park, Brig o'Turk, Callander

Public toilets
In Glen Finglas Gateway Centre (open Apr–Oct)

Cafés/pubs
Brig o'Turk Tearoom; Byre Inn, Brig o'Turk

Terrain
Gravel, stone and grass paths, with sections of wide, flat boardwalk

Hilliness
Ascent after ① then descent ③ to ⑤

Footwear
Winter 🥾
Spring/Summer/Autumn 👟

Did you know? The Tearoom in Brig o'Turk is 100 years old and starred in the 1959 film of John Buchan's classic novel *The 39 Steps*. The thriller starred Kenneth More as Richard Hannay, being pursued around iconic Scottish locations, such as the Forth Bridge. Depicted as The Gallows Café, the tearoom was portrayed as a popular stopping point for cyclists, which it still is. Hannay escaped by pedalling off hidden among a group of cyclists.

Local legend Between ❹ and ❼, on the minor road that leads through Brig o'Turk to Glen Finglas, a strange tree can be found. The sycamore is known as the Bicycle Tree and has protected status. The story goes that a young man conscripted to fight in World War I left his bicycle hanging on a branch. He never returned for it and over the decades the tree grew and absorbed the bike, leaving the handlebars sticking out.

🚌 **Public transport**
Demand Responsive Transport: phone 0844 567 5670 or email drt@ aberfoylecoaches. com to book lift to and from Brig o'Turk

♿ **Accessibility**
Wheelchair and pushchair friendly from ❸ to ❶ and then via pavement into Brig o'Turk, and along Glen Finglas Road to the Ruskin Viewpoint

🐕 **Dogs** Welcome. No stiles

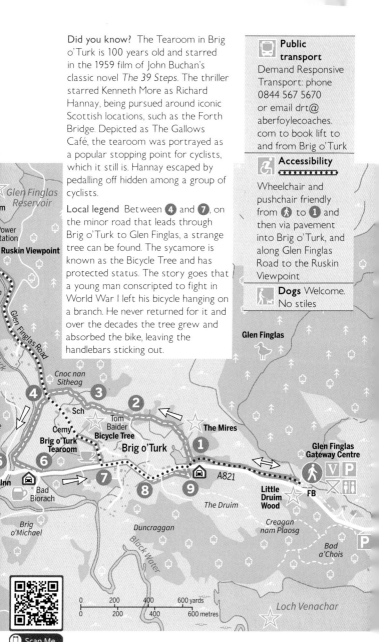

STORIES BEHIND
THE WALK

Glen Finglas At 12,044 acres, Glen Finglas is the Woodland Trust's largest site. The estate extends north and east from Brig o'Turk and includes many remnants of what was once continuous tree cover. It is part of the Great Trossachs Forest, a huge landscape-scale woodland restoration project stretching 30 miles from Loch Lomond to Callander. In the first 10 years of the 200-year project the Trust and neighbouring partners have planted more than two million native trees.

Little Druim Wood A path leads to a play and sculpture trail on the opposite side of the car park from the start of this walk. Designed to be fun for the family, it offers magic, music and dens set in beautiful ancient woodland. A leaflet (available in the car park) describes what you can see, and includes extra facts about the wildlife present and a quiz.

Glen Finglas

Little Druim Wood

The Mires

½ mil

Glen Finglas Gateway Centre
- Facing visitor centre, with your back to car park entrance, go **left** on path following blue arrows throughout.
- Walk parallel to road for ⅓ mile to gated boardwalk junction by main road.

1 - Go through first gate and turn **right** through second onto boardwalk across Brig o'Turk mires.
- Beyond bench viewpoint the surface changes to large cobblestones. Continue to T-junction.

❄ Ruskin Viewpoint A notable waterfall lies half a mile up Glen Finglas Road from **❹** – near the road head, branch left by a small car park to visit the falls. It was the backdrop for a famous portrait that the artist John Everett Millais painted in 1853 of the writer, naturalist and philosopher John Ruskin. Ruskin's wife, Effie Gray, accompanied them on this trip. Afterwards she had her marriage annulled for non-consummation and left him for Millais, with whom she had eight children.

☆ Water, water everywhere

The Trossachs landscape is one of rugged hills and sparkling lochs. Loch Venachar lies east of Brig o'Turk and Loch Achray is to the west. Glen Finglas Reservoir was built in 1958 so that water from the rivers Turk and Finglas could be piped to Loch Katrine, which is the source of Glasgow's water supply. The underground pipeline from the loch to the city was built in Victorian times and opened by Queen Victoria herself, in 1869.

🦆 Glen Finglas

➥ *For Ruskin Viewpoint, detour **right** up Glen Finglas Road (1 mile there and back).

❷ Steps

❸ Stepping stones

❄ Ruskin Viewpoint

❹ Steps | 1 mile

River Turk

❷ ➥ At junction go up stone steps and turn **right** through an open area.
➥ Descend to a metal gate with kissing-gate beside it.

❸ ➥ Go through, wind downhill and cross stepping stones over stream.
➥ Drop down to kissing-gate onto road with wooden fingerpost. *See detour, above.

NATURE NOTES

The Mires used to be a pond where the traditional winter sport of curling was practised when the ice was thick enough. The water was kept free of vegetation so that there was no impediment to the smooth glide of the stones. It is now a rich habitat for wildlife, including uncommon plants such as bogbean and marsh cinquefoil.

The small heath butterfly always lands with its wings closed and is well camouflaged against the grasses it inhabits, especially as it often hides the orange upper wing with an eyespot behind the brown lower one. It has declined by more than 50 per cent in the past 50 years, so is a conservation priority.

Wood anemones flower in early spring, often carpeting the woodland floor before trees shade the ground. They grow in ancient woodlands and are very slow to colonise new areas because they spread through the growth of their roots.

Highland cattle can usually be seen grazing on the south side of Loch Achray.

Above: Loch Achray
Opposite: **top**, small heath butterfly;
middle, wood anemone;
bottom, The Mires

Bicycle Tree
(200 yards left)

Brig o' Turk
Tearoom

Byre Inn; A821

7

The Rid

1½ miles

8

5

6

4 ➥ To continue route, go **straight across** the lane and down stone steps onto a fenced path.
➥ Walk between field and River Turk until path bends **left** in ¼ mile.

5 ➥ Cross track into field and keep **ahead** on path.
➥ Pass wooden barriers and cross road (A821) with care by entrance to Byre Inn.

6 ➥ Pass entrance and walk along pavement on right side of main road.
➥ Follow pavement for 375 yards to road junction.

Highland cow

Little Druim
Wood

9 A821

2 miles

Glen Finglas
Gateway Centre

➠ On the **left** is
the Brig o'Turk
Tearoom. To visit
the Bicycle Tree,
detour 200 yards up
Glen Finglas Road.
➠ Continue on main
road pavement
to house sign The
Ridings.

8 ➠ Here, the
pavement ends
and path continues
parallel to the road.
➠ Keep **ahead** over
a track to a junction
where pink-arrowed
route joins from gate
on right.

9 ➠ Zigzag **left** down
to gate and cross
road with care back
to **1**.
➠ Go through gate
on **right** and retrace
steps to car park.

WATERFALLS AND OAK COPPICE TRAILS

The views from The Lodge at the start of this walk are tremendous, stretching over the Highland edge to the Lowlands south of Aberfoyle. The route then descends through woodland to the foot of an impressive waterfall. On return, the choice is to stick to the wheelchair-friendly Waterfall Trail or take the rougher Oak Coppice Trail, which winds downstream through habitat rich in mosses, ferns and wildlife before climbing back up. Look out for red squirrels and roe deer.

OS information	
🚶 NN 520014	Explorer OL46

Distance
1.9 miles/3.1km

Time
1 hour

Start/Finish
The Lodge Forest Visitor Centre

Parking FK8 3SX
The Lodge, 1 mile north of Aberfoyle on A821 at start of the Duke's Pass

Public toilets
The Lodge

Cafés/pubs
Lodge Café; Aberfoyle

Terrain
Well-surfaced woodland path to ❺ then smaller, rougher path

Hilliness
Gradual descent to waterfall and after ❺ more downhill to ❼ then steeper climb back up

Footwear
Winter 🥾 Spring/Summer/ Autumn 👟

Did you know? The forest is home to one of the longest zip wires in Britain, which soars across the valley, passing above the waterfall visited on this walk. A part of the Go Ape adventure course, it is a dizzying 120 feet high and 466 yards long. Exploring the treetops while safely strapped into a harness is an exhilarating and memorable experience!

Local legend Aberfoyle once had a minister who was known to commune with fairies. In 1691, the Reverend Robert Kirk published *The Secret Commonwealth of Elves and Fairies*, and soon after he mysteriously disappeared. His body was found nearby on Doon Hill, leaning against a tree and dressed only in a nightgown. Many believed that the fairies killed him in revenge for revealing their secrets and that the tree is a doorway to an underground Fairy Queen's palace.

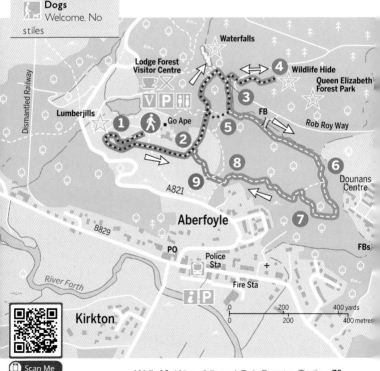

STORIES BEHIND THE WALK

☆ **Queen Elizabeth Forest Park**

The Lodge is the gateway to Queen Elizabeth Forest Park, established in 1953, the year of the coronation of Elizabeth II. The park extends from the eastern shores of Loch Lomond to the mountains of Strathyre. The Lodge opened in 1960 and was originally called David Marshall Lodge after the chairman of the Carnegie UK Trust, which helped fund its construction. It contains wildlife exhibitions and a café.

☆ **Lumberjills**

In World War II, with many men away fighting, there was a shortage of labour to harvest trees for pit props and other essential uses, so the Women's Timber Corps was created. This branch of the Women's Land Army started in 1942 when the German occupation of Norway caused a shortage of imported timber. The women were known as Lumberjills and a statue near ❶ commemorates their contribution to the war effort.

 Go Ape ☆ Lumberjills ❶ ☆ Queen Elizabeth Forest P

The Lodge Forest Visitor Centre

🠖 Take path from map boards on right of The Lodge and follow green-ringed posts of Oak Coppice Trail throughout.

🠖 Follow it to the statue dedicated to the Lumberjills above a picnic area.

❶ 🠖 Follow main, well-surfaced path for ¼ mile as it bends **left** downhill, ignoring rough side paths, to reach a fingerposted junction.

❷ 🠖 Keep **ahead** here (signed Aberfoyle to the right).

🠖 At wide junction with roe deer sculptures, turn **left**.

🠖 Cross a stretch of boardwalk to stream, where waterfall is on left, and walk downstream to footbridge.

☆ The Trossachs

The Trossachs is the narrow wooded valley between Loch Katrine and Loch Achray, but the name is now applied to the whole region between Aberfoyle and Callander. This area gained popularity as a Victorian tourist destination after Sir Walter Scott published *The Lady of the Lake* in 1810. The narrative poem sold 25,000 copies in eight months and many readers flocked here to enjoy the landscapes around Loch Katrine, where the action is set.

☆ Loch Katrine

Set amid rocky hills, this sparkling loch remains a popular tourist destination. Trossachs Pier is home to the *Sir Walter Scott* steamship, named after the writer. Sightseeing cruises take in Ellen's Isle, named after Scott's heroine, and Queen Victoria's Cottage, built for her visit in 1869. Alternatively, you can sail to Stronachlachar at the far end and walk or cycle back on the private road along the north side of the loch. A shorter waymarked walk goes to Brenachoile viewpoint.

☆ Waterfalls (left)   ☆ Wildlife hide

½ mile

Wheelchairs should follow
Waterfall Trail back to The Lodge

3 ➡ **Cross** footbridge to track junction and go **straight across** on path with binoculars symbol.
➡ It winds under tall conifers to a wildlife hide, where red squirrels and birds visit feeders.

4 ➡ Retrace steps to footbridge and turn **left** on downstream path, past information board about stream's name.
➡ Pass a play area with sluices to a junction where easier Waterfall Trail (white-ringed post) goes ahead back to The Lodge.

NATURE NOTES

Oak coppice is created by cutting down trees so that multiple stems re-grow from a single stump. Done repeatedly every 15 to 20 years it generates fresh timber without replanting and can extend a tree's life almost indefinitely.

The wildlife hide at ❹ is a great place for watching red squirrels visiting the special feeders. These have lids to stop birds raiding them. Young squirrels soon learn to lift the lids to take nuts, which they often sit and eat on the ledge before darting off in a flash of fur.

A distinctive bird that can be seen from the hide is the nuthatch, with its blue-grey back, orange-buff chest and black line through the eye. It is able to walk down tree trunks head first. Milder winters have allowed the nuthatch to spread north – it was unknown here 20 years ago. Coal tits are the most numerous visitors to the bird feeders.

The small tortoiseshell overwinters as an adult and is one of the first butterflies of spring.

Pussy willow is so named because the male catkins of the goat willow look like a cat's paws before they open and shed pollen.

Oak copplce

Dounans Centre (glimpsed through trees)	☆ Queen Elizabeth Forest Park
1 mile ❻	❼ Steps

❺ ➡ Turn **left** (green- and red-ringed post) to stay close to stream on rougher path.
➡ Where the red trail goes left across another footbridge, keep **ahead** to a sign about oak coppicing.

❻ ➡ Continue past sign, and keep **ahead** over slight rise where Dounans Centre is visible across burn.
➡ Turn sharp **right** at a post (minor path goes left) and keep **ahead** until path forks.

Top left: nuthatch
Top right: red squirrel
Above: frog
Left: coal tit

Go Ape
2 miles

The Lodge Forest
Visitor Centre

½ miles

9

➤ Go **right**, up stone steps to a T-junction and turn **left** downhill past a seat.
➤ After the zigzag downhill, bear **right** beside little stream then keep **right**, uphill, to junction.

8 ➤ Turn **left** by post with orange and white orienteering symbol.
➤ At junction with fingerpost, turn **right**, signed The Lodge, and climb to crossroads with tarmac cycle path.

9 ➤ Go **diagonally across**, signed The Lodge, and climb up to fingerpost at **2**.
➤ Turn **left** and retrace your steps back to start.

Publishing information

© Crown copyright 2023.
All rights reserved.

Ordnance Survey, OS, and the OS logos are registered trademarks, and OS Short Walks Made Easy is a trademark of Ordnance Survey Ltd.

© Crown copyright and database rights (2023) Ordnance Survey.

ISBN 978 0 319092 66 8
1st edition published by Ordnance Survey 2023.

www.ordnancesurvey.co.uk

While every care has been taken to ensure the accuracy of the route directions, the publishers cannot accept responsibility for errors or omissions, or for changes in details given. The countryside is not static: hedges and fences can be removed, stiles can be replaced by gates, field boundaries can alter, footpaths can be rerouted and changes in ownership can result in the closure or diversion of some concessionary paths. Also, paths that are easy and pleasant for walking in fine conditions may become slippery, muddy and difficult in wet weather.

If you find an inaccuracy in either the text or maps, please contact Ordnance Survey at os.uk/contact.

A catalogue record for this book is available from the British Library.

Milestone Publishing credits

Author: Felicity Martin

Series editor: Kevin Freeborn

Maps: Cosmographics

Design and Production: Patrick Dawson, Milestone Publishing

Printed in India by Replika Press Pvt. Ltd

Photography credits

Front cover: ©Felicity Martin
Back cover cornfield/Shutterstock.com.

All photographs supplied by the author ©Felicity Martin except page 6 Bee Leask and page 59 ppn2047/Shutterstock.com.